# STEP-by-STEP

## GEOGRAPHY

# Rivers and Lakes

Helena Ramsay

Illustrated by Roger Stewart
and Shirley Tourret

# W

# FRANKLIN WATTS

LONDON • NEW YORK • SYDNEY

© 1996 Franklin Watts

First published in Great Britain by
Franklin Watts
96 Leonard Street
London
EC2A 4RH

Franklin Watts Australia
14 Mars Road
Lane Cove
NSW 2006
Australia

ISBN: 0 7496 2393 4
10 9 8 7 6 5 4 3 2
Dewey Decimal Classification 551.48
A CIP catalogue record for this book is available from the British Library

Printed in Dubai

Planning and production by The Creative Publishing Company
Designed by Ian Winton
Edited by Patience Coster
Consultant: Keith Lye

Photographs: Bruce Coleman: page 6 (Jane Burton), 11 (Jules Cowan),
20 (Julie Fryer), 21 (C C Lockwood), 24 (Atlantide SDF), 26 (Gene Ahrens);
Frank Lane Picture Agency: page 5 (Richhorn/Eingel), 9 (M J Thomas); Natural History Photo
Agency: page 17 (Haroldo Palo), 23 (R Thwaites), 28 (B & C Alexander); Oxford Scientific Films:
page 8 (Deni Bown), 12, top (Richard Packwood), 12-13, bottom (John Mitchell), 14 (Belinda Wright);
Range/Bettmann/Reuters: page 30 (Sue Ogrocki); Tony Stone Worldwide:
page 15 (Nigel Press), 27 (Peter/Stef Lamberti), 18.

# Contents

# Moving Water

There are many rivers in the world. Each one follows its own special journey. Rivers, like people, go through different stages in their lives. We talk about 'young' rivers, and rivers in 'old age'.

In the hills the young river is small, but the water flows swiftly and is powerful. The valley is narrow with steep sides.

This river is flowing down a **valley** from the mountains to the sea. Most river journeys end in the sea, but some end in lakes instead.

Lower down, other rivers join the **mature** river. It travels more slowly and its valley is wider.

## What are Lakes?

Lakes are formed when hollows in the Earth's surface fill up with water. They are often rich in wildlife. This is a photo of Lake Jipe in Africa, the home of many rare birds.

The old river is nearing the end of its journey. The valley is very wide. The flat land on either side of the river is the **flood plain**.

# Where Water Comes From

All living things need water to survive. But there is only a limited amount of water in the world. We use this water again and again, because of a process called the water cycle.

Rain falls from the clouds and fills rivers

As the sun shines down on the sea, some of the water **evaporates** to form **water vapour**. This is made of water that is invisible, like a gas. The vapour rises up into the sky, carried by **air currents**.

High above the Earth the air cools, and the invisible vapour turns back into tiny, visible droplets of water.

Vapour turns into water droplets which form clouds

Water vapour rises into the sky

The water droplets form clouds. In the clouds, the droplets merge to make raindrops, which are blown along by the wind. The water falls as rain on to the ground below, where it fills rivers, streams and lakes. These feed back into the sea, and the process begins again. This is the water cycle.

# The Young River

All rivers begin in a small way. The start of a river is called the source. Look at the picture. Here the source of the river is in the hills.

Sandstone

## From Spring to Stream

Many rivers start as springs, where water runs out of the ground. Long ago, springs were thought to be magical places.

When rain falls on to the ground it soaks into the soil and rocks. Some rocks, like sandstone, let the water through.

Clay

The water seeps through until it reaches a different type of rock, such as clay, that won't let the water through.

The young stream rushes and tumbles over its rocky **bed**. Rainwater and melted snow trickle off the hillside and other streams flow into it. As more streams join together, they become a river.

The water seeps along the clay and out into the open again.

# Changing the Landscape

On its journey, the river changes the landscape by flowing through it. The water carries worn bits of rock, such as mud, **silt**, sand and small stones.

River flows in this direction

Stones bounce over each other along the river bed

The river rolls and tumbles large stones and rocks which wear away the river bed like sandpaper. This is called **erosion**.

## MAKE A RIVER ON A PILE OF SAND

**1** If you have a sandpit outdoors, pile up some sand into a mound and push small stones into it.

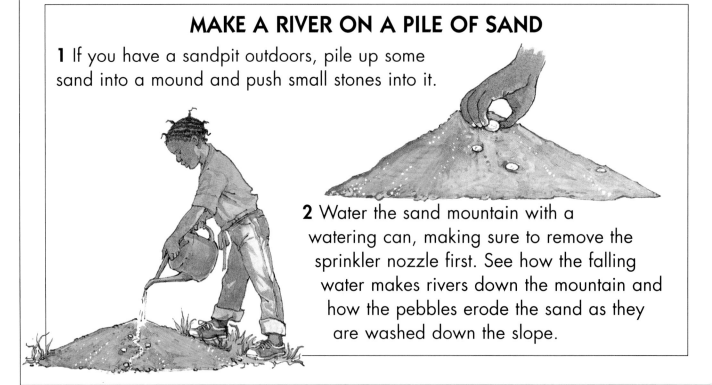

**2** Water the sand mountain with a watering can, making sure to remove the sprinkler nozzle first. See how the falling water makes rivers down the mountain and how the pebbles erode the sand as they are washed down the slope.

Sometimes the river cuts a deep valley with almost vertical sides. This is called a **gorge** or **canyon**.

## The Deepest Valleys

The Grand Canyon in the United States is an enormous gorge. In places it is 1.6 kilometres deep. The rocks have been worn away over thousands of years by the Colorado River.

The world's tallest building is the CN Tower in Toronto, Canada. This picture shows that the depth of the Grand Canyon is three times greater than the height of the CN Tower.

# Rapids and Waterfalls

During its journey a river may suddenly become steeper or narrower. **Rapids** form where the water travels very fast.

When the river water reaches a steep drop, it becomes a waterfall. Mountain rivers often have many waterfalls.

The world's highest falls are the Angel Falls in the South American jungle. Here the water plunges nearly 1,000 metres.

## Frozen Falls

The Niagara Falls are on the border between Canada and the United States. In winter it is sometimes so cold there that the moving water freezes.

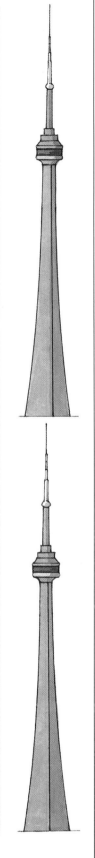

The Angel Falls are nearly twice as tall as the CN Tower, the world's tallest building.

# The River in Old Age

As the river nears the end of its journey it becomes wider and slower moving. It has now reached the flat land and is winding its way to the sea. An old river tends to make S-shaped bends like this. These bends are called meanders.

The point where the river flows into the sea is known as the mouth. If the river has a wide mouth, this is called an estuary.

mouth

estuary

As it meets the sea, the river drops its load of mud, silt and sand which spreads out over the sea bed. Sometimes, if the tides are not strong, the silt piles up around the river mouth. The river breaks up into many smaller **channels** that run through the silt. The silt forms new land, called a delta.

## Where River Meets Sea

This photo, taken from space, shows the triangular shape of a delta. This is the delta of the River Nile in Egypt.

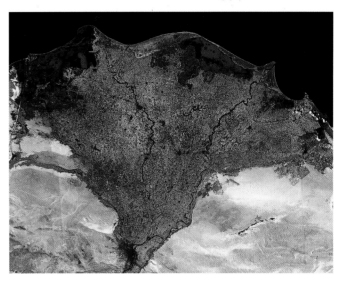

## MAKE SOME SILT!

**1** Collect **a)** some fine mud, **b)** some soil, and **c)** some sand.

**2** Mix sample **a)** with a little tap water. Pour this muddy water into a jam-jar and leave until the water has cleared. The mud will sink to the bottom.

**3** Repeat stage 2 with the other samples. Pour each one carefully on top of the last. Be careful not to shake the jar. See how the samples build up in layers. This is how silt is formed.

# Underground Rivers

Sometimes rivers flow into holes in the ground called swallow holes. The water runs down into caves and tunnels to form underground lakes and rivers.

These stalactites and stalagmites have been made by water dripping through the cave roof and on to the cave floor. The water evaporates, leaving very thin layers of rock. These build up over many years to form stalactites hanging down from the roof and stalagmites growing up from the floor.

# Rivers of Ice

Glaciers are moving rivers of ice. They form high up in the mountains when layers of snow fall into a valley. The snow on the ground is gradually pressed to ice as more snow falls on top. The glacier slides slowly down the side of the mountain.

Some glaciers end in the sea. Large pieces break away from the edge of the glacier and float away as icebergs.

Thousands of years ago, the world was much colder than it is now. We call this period the Ice Age. There were many more glaciers during this time than there are now.

### Ice Man

In 1991, some people found the body of a man in the front edge of a glacier. He had been frozen in the ice about 7,000 years ago.

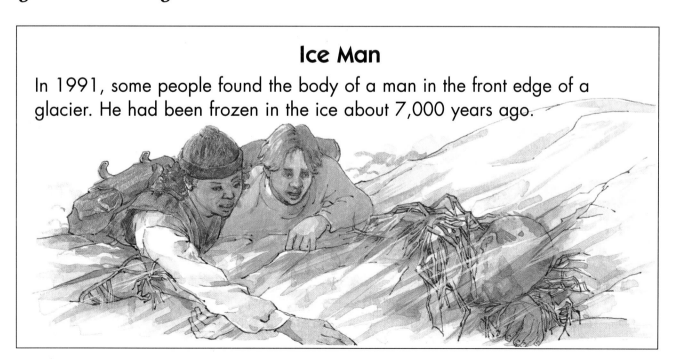

# How Lakes are Made

Lakes are made in many different ways. They often form where rivers have become blocked by mud or rocks. These huge dams stop the water from flowing away.

Sometimes water collects in hollows in the land made when glaciers scraped away the rock many thousands of years ago.

Lakes are also made by people and animals. **Beavers** build dams of logs, stones and mud in woodland streams.

The dam blocks the stream and makes a lake in which the beavers build their homes.

# A Volcanic Lake

This is Crater Lake in the United States. It was made when rain and snow fell into the crater of an **extinct** volcano.

## MAKE A POND

**1** Dig a hole in the ground. Make it about half a metre deep and 1 metre across. The sides should slope gently.

**2** Make sure there are no stones in the pond, then line it with a sheet of tough plastic. The plastic must overlap the edge.

**3** Put some sifted soil into the pond. Plant small water lilies, marsh marigolds and watermint in the soil. Fill your pond with water, and wait for the birds, frogs and insects to arrive!

# Lakes and Rivers Everywhere

This map shows the most important rivers and lakes in the world. Can you find the world's longest river? It flows for over 6,000 kilometres through north-east Africa.

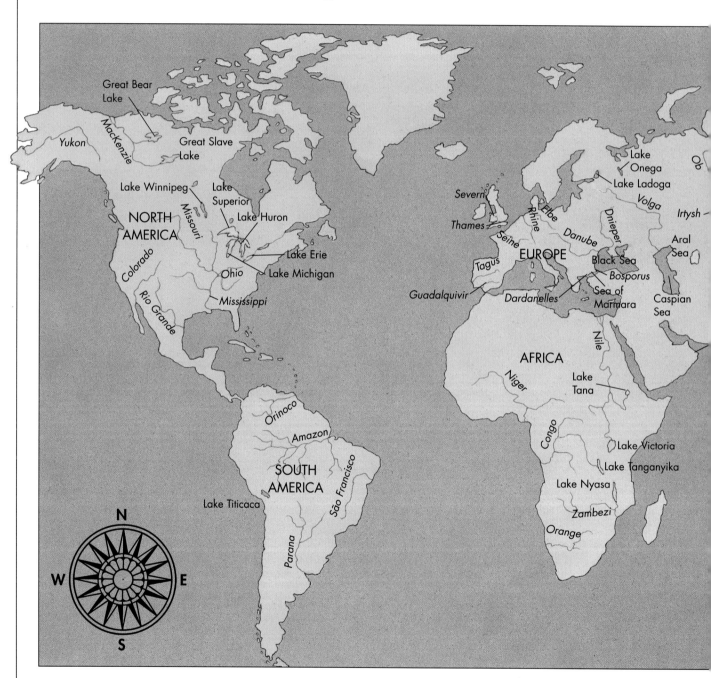

## A Dry Lake

When it is full, Lake Eyre is the largest lake in Australia. But it only fills up during very wet weather. For most of the year the lake is dry. Its surface is covered by a crust of salt 4.5 metres thick.

The Amazon contains more water than any other river. Can you find it on the map?

The deepest lake in the world is Lake Baikal. Can you find it?

The biggest lake in the world is in western Asia. It is a saltwater lake called the Caspian Sea. Salt lakes are found in the hot, dry parts of the world. The water can't escape from these lakes, so the **minerals** from the rocks around them are trapped, making the water salty.

# Living by Water

The world's most important cities are often built beside rivers or lakes, because people have always needed water in their everyday lives. This photo shows the River Arno running through the city of Florence in Italy.

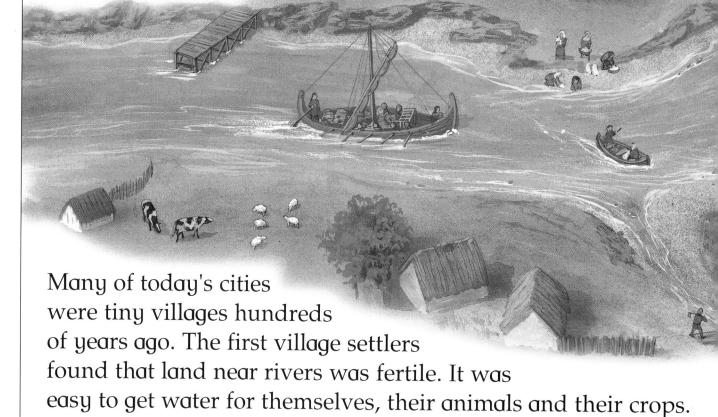

Many of today's cities were tiny villages hundreds of years ago. The first village settlers found that land near rivers was fertile. It was easy to get water for themselves, their animals and their crops.

Rivers were also good for transport. The early settlers travelled along the river by boat. There were few roads in those days, and this was the easiest way for them to journey from place to place.

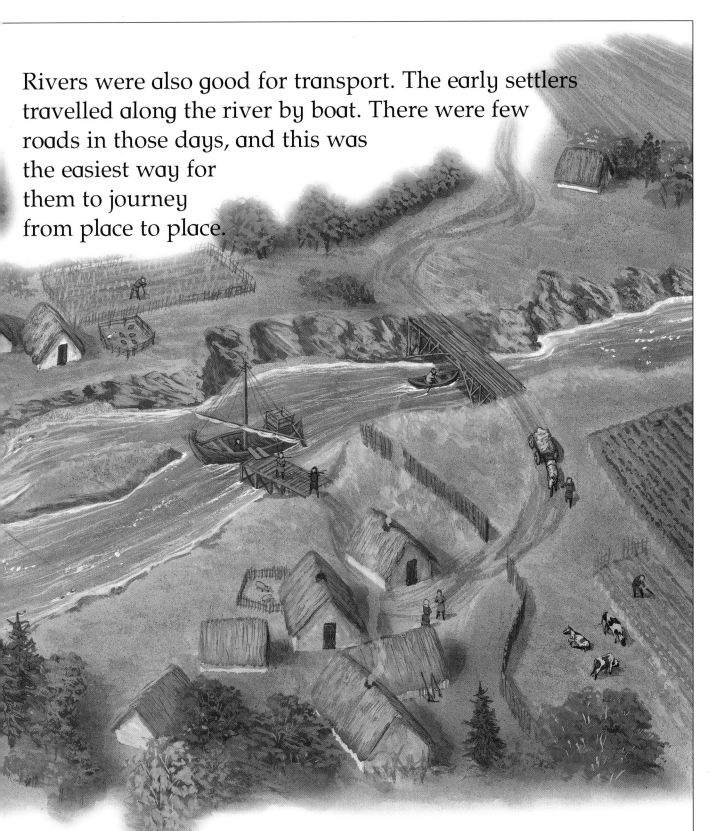

In order to get from one side of the river to the other, people built bridges. The first bridges were made from tree trunks.

# Water Power

Running water is very powerful. For hundreds of years it has been used to drive machinery. Waterwheels were first used to power machines for grinding wheat.

## MAKE A WATERWHEEL

**1** Ask an adult to help you cut the foil lid from a large yogurt pot. Make a small hole in the middle of the lid.

**2** Cutting only up to two-thirds of the way in, make eight slits in the lid. Fold the edges over, first one way, then the other.

**3** Push a pencil through the hole. Hold your wheel under a gently running tap and see it spin round.

Water can be used to make electricity. **Hydro-electric dams** block the flow of rivers and channel the water to turn giant wheels called turbines. The turbines turn the generators that make electricity.

# Making Water Work

This is the Hoover hydro-electric Dam in the United States. The valley behind this dam has filled with water to create a reservoir, or **artificial** lake.

# Rivers, Lakes and People

People use lakes and rivers in many ways. They depend on them for water and fish in them for food. Sometimes they **extract** minerals from silt under the water. Rivers are still used today to transport passengers and cargo.

## Water as a Way of Life

All over the world people fish in rivers and lakes. This Inuit man is fishing through a hole in the ice.

Lakes and rivers are used for all kinds of leisure activities too. What are the people using water for in this picture?

# River Disasters

After heavy rain, rivers sometimes flood. Flooding causes terrible damage. The Mississippi River in the United States flooded large areas in 1993. Hundreds of homes were destroyed.

Many factories are built beside rivers. If dirty water is allowed to pour out of a factory into a river, it can **pollute** it. We can too, if we carelessly throw rubbish into rivers.

Rivers can be polluted by water running off fields that have been treated with chemical fertilizers. One of the most dangerous forms of pollution is **sewage**. This should be carefully treated before being released into rivers.

Pollution kills the fish, animals and plants living in the water. We must make sure that our rivers and lakes are kept clean and free from pollution.

# Glossary

**Air current:** A flow of air

**Artificial:** Made by humans

**Beavers:** Animals with broad tails and brown fur that live both on land and in water

**Bed:** The bottom of a river or sea

**Canyon:** A long, narrow valley between high cliffs

**Channels:** Small tracks through which water flows

**Erosion:** Wearing away

**Evaporate:** To change into vapour

**Extinct:** No longer active

**Extract:** To take out

**Flood plain:** A plain along a river, made from river mud left behind after flooding

**Gorge:** A deep, narrow pass between high cliffs

**Hydro-electric dam:** A dam used to make electricity from water power

**Mature:** Fully grown

**Minerals:** Substances like copper, iron, zinc etc. that are present in the earth

**Pollute:** To make dirty

**Rapids:** Part of a river that flows very swiftly

**Sewage:** Waste matter produced by people

**Silt:** Part of the river's load, made up of grains smaller than sand but larger than clay

**Valley:** Low land between hills or mountains

**Water vapour:** Invisible moisture in the air

# Index